THE NEW TESTAMENT DEACON

ABOUT THE AUTHOR:

Alexander Strauch resides with his wife and two teenage daughters in Littleton, Colorado, and also has two married daughters in the area. Mr. Strauch is a gifted Bible teacher and an elder in a church in Littleton, Colorado, where he has served for the past twenty-seven years. Other works by Mr. Strauch include:

Men and Women: Equal Yet Different

The New Testament Deacon: Study Guide

Biblical Eldership:
An Urgent Call to Restore Biblical Church Leadership

Study Guide to Biblical Eldership:
Twelve Lessons for Mentoring Men for Eldership

The Mentor's Guide to Biblical Eldership:
Twelve Lessons for Mentoring Men for Eldership
(co-authored with Richard Swartley)

Biblical Eldership:
Restoring the Eldership to its Rightful Place in the Church

The Hospitality Commands:
Building Loving Christian Community;
Building Bridges to Friends and Neighbors

Agape Leadership:
Lessons in Spiritual Leadership from the Life of R.C. Chapman
(co-authored with Robert Peterson)

ALEXANDER STRAUCH

THE NEW TESTAMENT DEACON

THE CHURCH'S MINISTER OF MERCY

LEWIS AND ROTH PUBLISHERS
P.O. Box 569, Littleton, Colorado 80160 U.S.A.
www.lewisandroth.org

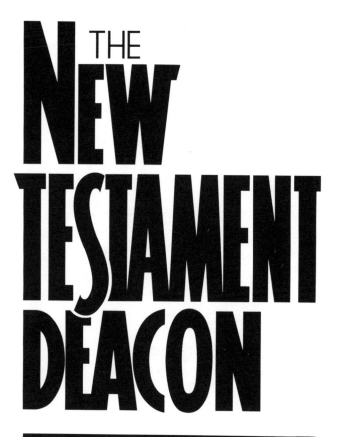

FOR A FREE CATALOG OF OTHER BOOKS PUBLISHED BY LEWIS AND ROTH PUBLISHERS, WRITE, CALL OR VISIT OUR WEBSITE:

LEWIS AND ROTH PUBLISHERS
P.O. BOX 569
LITTLETON, COLORADO 80160-0569 U.S.A.
www.lewisandroth.org
CALL TOLL FREE 1-800-477-3239
(U.S.A./CANADA)

(303) 794-3239 (LOCAL/INTERNATIONAL)

Cover Design: Stephen T. Eames

Library of Congress Cataloging-in-Publication Data

Strauch, Alexander, 1944-
The New Testament deacon: the church's minister of mercy/
Alexander Strauch.
p. cm.
Includes bibliographical references and indexes.
ISBN 0-936083-07-7
1. Deacons—Biblical teaching. 2. Bible. N.T.—Criticism, interpretation, etc. I. Title.
BS2545.D4S77 1992
262'.14'09015—dc20 92-29609
CIP

Printed in the United States of America

05 04 03 02 9

ISBN 0-936083-07-7

Contents

ACKNOWLEDGMENTS

I am grateful to many dear Christian friends for helping to make this book possible.

I especially thank those who took time out of their busy schedules to interact with me and sharpen my understanding of the texts of holy Scripture. Of those, I personally thank David Gooding, George W. Knight III, Craig Van Schooneveld, Mark Smith, Jack Fish, David MacLeod, and Darrel Bock.

In preparing this book for print, I had many willing helpers: Stephen and Amanda Sorenson, my editors; Maggie Crossett; Allegra James; Barbara Peek; and my wife, Marilyn.

Facing the Issues

When writing to Timothy and the problem-ridden congregation at Ephesus around the year A.D. 63, Paul found it necessary to give instructions about deacons. In 1 Timothy 3:8-13, he insists that deacons, like shepherds, be properly qualified and publicly examined before they serve. Since he did not want their position to be minimized by others or by themselves, Paul promises that deacons who serve well will acquire an honorable and influential standing in the local church. They will also see their faith in Christ greatly increased. He writes, "For those who have served well as deacons obtain for themselves a high standing and great confidence in the faith that is in Christ Jesus" (1 Timothy 3:13).

But who are these deacons who gain "a high standing and great confidence in the faith"? What do they do? Why are they important to the life of the local church?

Intense interest surrounds these questions today. During the last three decades, a major revival of interest in deacons has taken place. In nearly every denomination and branch of Christianity, efforts are underway to discover God's design for deacons.[1] One study on the diaconate concluded, "The church across the world is in ferment with new thinking about the diaconate as an office of ministry."[2] (The word *diaconate* denotes the office of deacon.)

We must be grateful for all that is good in these efforts and be glad to learn from them. But a serious, fundamental problem regarding the diaconate still exists: *far too little in-depth consideration is being given to the biblical texts and the biblical parameters set for deacons.* This problem is symptomatic of a much bigger problem among Christians today, which is a shameful lack of trust in God-breathed, holy Scripture. But, as we shall see, the Scripture is perfectly sufficient to answer our questions about deacons. Indeed, the only diaconate worth discovering is the one found on the pages of the inspired New Testament. No matter how limited that information may at first appear, God, in His perfect wisdom, has given us all the information we need.

If we don't adequately consider the texts of holy Scripture or limit ourselves to biblical teaching on deacons, we invariably corrupt God's design and invent a diaconate of our own imagination. Consider the following three common distortions of the New Testament diaconate.

Ruling Executives

Many Bible-believing churches (churches to which this book is primarily aimed) have made the diaconate the ruling board of the church. Richard L. Dresselhaus, writing from an Assembly of God perspective, calls the diaconate "the official board" of the church.[3] He also states,

> One of the most awesome responsibilities of the deacon board is to provide continued pastoral ministry in the church. When a pastor resigns, it becomes their responsibility to present to the congregation a nominee or nominees to fill the office of pastor."[4]

In many churches, deacons act more like corporation executives than ministering servants. In direct contradiction to the explicit teaching of the New Testament and the very meaning of the name *deacon,* which is "servant" (*diakonos*), deacons have been made the governing officials of the church.

Even more troublesome is the fact that deacons are often placed into a competitive role with the shepherds of the local church. This practice is a proven formula for prolonged church warfare. (For the sake of communicating to readers from various denominational backgrounds, I use the terms *shepherds, pastors, elders*, and *overseers* interchangeably to describe the same pastoral body. See chapter 5, pages 60-68)

Building and Property Managers

While some churches wrongly elevate deacons to the position of executive board members, others mistakenly reduce deacons to building managers, glorified church janitors, or sanctified groundskeepers. This view (and a similar view that turns deacons into church financial officers) seriously demeans the office of deacon and denies the local church the necessary ministry God designed the diaconate to provide for His people.

In response to this position, we must ask ourselves why God would demand that deacons meet specific moral and spiritual qualifications and undergo public examination, like the pastors of the church (1 Timothy 3:10), if all deacons do is wax floors or mow lawns. Anyone in the church, or even people outside the church, can do these types of jobs.

The Church Factotums

Southern Baptist scholar Charles W. Deweese makes the deacon the church factotum, that is, an official who operates in nearly every area of church life:

> The potential areas of deacon service are unlimited. Deacons can engage in such diverse ministries as teaching, preaching, visiting, becoming involved in social action, counseling, leading in charitable giving, organizing, administrating, carrying out the Lord's Supper, and meeting basic needs of the pastor.[5]

Such unlimited spheres of service completely blur the distinctive purpose and duties of the New Testament diaconate and can only frustrate deacons.

In their zeal for deacon renewal, many churches have gone too far, beyond the bounds of Scripture. They have placed too much authority and diverse responsibilities into the hands of deacons. In fact, some of the same mistakes that churches made in the middle of the second century are being made again: deacons are placed in various positions of authority that God has not authorized.[6] Hopefully this book will help correct the many exaggerated claims being made today about the role of deacons.

MINISTERS OF MERCY

My heartfelt burden is to help deacons get out of the boardroom or the building-maintenance mentality and into the people-serving mentality. Deacons, as the New Testament teaches and as some of the sixteenth-century reformers discovered,[7] are to be involved in a compassionate ministry of caring for the poor and needy. *The deacons' ministry, therefore, is one that no Christ-centered, New Testament church can ever afford to neglect.*

Christians today must understand the absolute necessity for and vital importance of New Testament deacons to the local church so that the needy, poor, and suffering of our churches are cared for in a thoroughly Christian manner. This is a matter dear to the heart of God.

Stressing the significance of our responsibility to the poor, the brilliant, eighteenth-century, American pastor- theologian, Jonathan Edwards (1703-1758) wrote: "I know of scarce any duty which is so much insisted on, so pressed and urged upon us, both in the Old Testament and New, as this duty of charity to the poor."[8]

So often, however, churches neglect poor and needy people. Churches spend hundreds of thousands of dollars—even millions—on buildings, draperies, pews, and stained glass windows, but can barely squeeze a thousand dollars out of their budgets to help their own needy people.

God has given deacons a wonderful ministry of service, mercy, and love to needy people. Indeed, deacons are to emulate our Lord's example of humble, loving service to needy people. Our Lord highly esteems the deacons' work, for it is essential to the life and witness of God's church. Thus we urgently need to rediscover and put into practice a New Testament diaconate. Toward this effort I will seek to explain who the New Testament deacons are and what they do. I will do this through a careful, thorough exposition of all the biblical passages that relate to deacons.

A Call to Obedience for Shepherds and Deacons

Obedience to Scripture does not come naturally, yet it is the indispensable basis of Christian living and the basis for the local church's growth, direction, correction, and revival. I recognize that most deacons will resist change, especially if they hold a position of power. So I can only pray that the Holy Spirit of God will use the Word of God, accurately and thoroughly expounded, to affect needed change in the thinking of many deacons.

This book is also aimed at showing the shepherds of the church their need for deacons and their responsibilities toward them. For in order for deacons to do their work effectively, they need the guidance and support that only the shepherds of the church can provide. Unfortunately, many churches and their leaders are uncertain about the need for deacons.[9] Some churches don't even have deacons. Yet church shepherds today desperately need the deacons to relieve them from the many practical care needs essential to shepherding a flock so that the shepherds can attend more fully to teaching, guarding, and leading the whole flock. So I hope this book will help people think more biblically about the diaconate and become more willing to change church structures that are not biblically based.

*

Because this book is a biblical examination and exposition of all New Testament texts on deacons, I have not addressed many practical issues concerning the implementation and operation of the diaconate. Instead, I have prepared a separate guide book to deal with these practical issues related to the implementation of a New Testament diaconate. You can order the guide book to *The New Testament Deacon* from Lewis and Roth Publishers or your favorite book store.

Part One

DIVIDING UP THE WORK: WORD AND DEED

"Give us this day our daily bread."

Matthew 6:11

This is pure and undefiled religion in the sight of our God and Father, to visit orphans and widows in their distress, and to keep oneself unstained by the world.

James 1:27

He has told you, O man, what is good;
And what does the Lord require of you
But to do justice, *to love kindness,*
And to walk humbly with your God?

Micah 6:8; italics added

James and Cephas and John, who were reputed to be pillars, gave to me and Barnabas the right hand of fellowship...they only asked us to remember the poor—the very thing I also was eager to do.

Galatians 2:9*b*,10

Chapter 1

The Shepherds' Priorities: Word and Prayer

> **Now at this time while the disciples were increasing in number, a complaint arose on the part of the Hellenistic Jews against the native Hebrews, because their widows were being overlooked in the daily serving of food. And the twelve summoned the congregation of the disciples and said, "It is not desirable for us to neglect the word of God in order to serve tables. But select from among you, brethren, seven men of good reputation, full of the Spirit and of wisdom, whom we may put in charge of this task. But we will devote ourselves to prayer, and to the ministry of the word."**
>
> **Acts 6:1-4**

In terms of church leadership, Acts 6 is one of the most significant passages in the New Testament and should be ranked alongside Paul's message to the Ephesian elders (Acts 20:17-38) for its relevance to church pastors. Church shepherds should read Acts 6 every six months, for it is packed to overflowing with rich truths and dynamic lessons about church leadership and spiritual priorities. It emphasizes the centrality of the Word of God and the need to care for the poor. It addresses issues of conflict and problem solving, leadership character, finances, prayer, evangelism, love, humility, and community. It also directly addresses the subject of deacons.

In order to understand the role of the New Testament deacon, we must begin by understanding the shepherds' role in the church. In both places in Scripture where the title *deacon* appears, it is intimately associated with the shepherds of the church (see Philippians 1:1; 1 Timothy 3:8-13). Acts 6, which does not actually mention the word *deacon*, reveals why the office of deacon was created. It resulted from a two-fold need: to relieve the shepherds so that they can give priority time and attention to the Word and prayer, and to provide official, responsible care for the physical welfare of needy believers.

The apostles themselves eloquently state the need for shepherds to be relieved of the many practical care needs of the congregation (Acts 6:2,4). In Acts 6:2 the apostles state the need negatively: "It is not desirable for us to neglect the word of God in order to serve tables." Then, in Acts 6:4 the apostles state the need positively: "But we will devote ourselves to prayer, and to the ministry of the word."

Let's look carefully at these critically significant passages of Scripture. In this chapter we will expound the shepherds' priorities, for they are essential to understanding the role of the New Testament deacon.

In the following chapter we will explore the task given to the Seven, the forerunners to later deacons. We will conclude this section with a defense of Acts 6 as the origin of the New Testament diaconate.

Conflict Over the Poor

> Now at this time while the disciples were increasing in number, a complaint arose on the part of the Hellenistic Jews against the native Hebrews, because their widows were being overlooked in the daily serving of food (Acts 6:1).

The apostles constituted the first official leadership body of the first Christian congregation. The Twelve, as Luke calls them, were the church's body of overseers or shepherds.

They were responsible not only for the teaching and overall pastoral oversight of the congregation, but also for the collection and distribution of the church's funds for the poor (Acts 4:32-5:11). These responsibilities soon proved to be overwhelming.

The church in Jerusalem was growing quickly. Of course this growth was good. The Spirit of God was mightily at work in Jerusalem, and many people were being converted. The church was not only growing in size, but its social character was changing. A great number of Hellenistic Jews began to enter the company of disciples. Hellenistic Jews were Greek-speaking Jews who had immigrated to Jerusalem from foreign lands and who were often culturally and ideologically broader in outlook than the Aramaic-speaking, Palestinian Jews. Because of these differences, the Hellenistic Jews naturally formed a socially distinct group. This made them somewhat suspect by the more conservative, "native Hebrews," who were native-born, Aramaic-speaking Jews.

Despite the Christians' generous display of charity, a divisive problem arose among the Hellenistic and Hebrew believers. When it came to the distribution of funds or food, Hellenistic widows were repeatedly neglected. The Hebrew Christians, who were the more dominant group, controlled the funds, so the Hellenistic Jews started to grumble against them.

Here was the congregation's first big test of brotherly love. Could these Christians solve their cultural and attitudinal differences? Would their Christian love transcend age-old cultural and social prejudices, or would pride and fear cause division, as it so often does? Would the Holy Spirit of God be grieved by their fighting? Would their Christian witness be marred? Something had to be done or the church would split apart.

The Apostles Take Action

And the twelve summoned the congregation of the disciples

> and said, "It is not desirable for us to neglect the word of God in order to serve tables. But select from among you, brethren, seven men of good reputation, full of the Spirit and of wisdom, whom we may put in charge of this task. But we will devote ourselves to prayer, and to the ministry of the word" (Acts 6:2-4).

Good leaders always distinguish themselves by their ability to skillfully confront troublesome issues and to be decisive. In fact, confronting problems is a major part of leadership responsibility. Fearful leaders who refuse to confront problems have demoralized many churches and organizations. Running away from problems creates worse problems. In this trying situation facing the Jerusalem church, the apostles acted decisively and skillfully. Their actions avoided a potential disaster and led to the creation of a better situation.

Summoning the congregation, the apostles first declared their frustration with the situation. They began by saying, "'It is not desirable for us to neglect the word of God in order to serve tables.'" This does not mean the apostles disliked caring for widows, nor does it imply that they thought they were too important for such work. Not at all! They had truly learned from Jesus to be merciful and compassionate. For three years they had daily observed Jesus' burning compassion for the needy. From the first days after Pentecost, the apostles gladly served the poor and the sick (Acts 4:34-37; 5:16). However, caring for poor and sick people was not the apostles' first, God-given priority. Indeed, caring for needy people could divert them from their primary responsibility of proclaiming the cross of Christ.

The apostles have no doubt about their calling. They are quite emphatic in saying, "'It is not desirable for us to neglect the word of God.'" "Desirable" is the *New American Standard Bible's* rendering of the Greek word *arestos* that often means "pleasing" (cf. Acts 12:3). However, the word *pleasing* in this context probably is better translated as "right."

The apostles feel strongly about this matter. They know it is not right that they neglect preaching the Word in order to serve widows. Although caring for widows is important, the apostles know they must not allow even this honorable service to divert them from proclaiming and teaching the Word of the living God. That would be disastrous.

We all know we need food in order to live. That is why we expend so much energy to provide food for ourselves. Yet, most people don't know that they also need the Word of God in order to live. In the Old Testament, Moses told Israel, "'... [God] let you be hungry, and fed you with manna which you did not know...that He might make you understand that man does not live by bread alone, but man lives by everything that proceeds out of the mouth of the Lord'" (Deuteronomy 8:3). Our Lord also said, "'Do not work for the food which perishes, but for the food which endures to eternal life, which the Son of Man shall give to you'" (John 6:27).

People cannot truly live without God's Word. They cannot experience life as God intended it without believing the message of salvation through Jesus Christ. Nothing could be more important to the lost sons and daughters of Adam than God's message of salvation. That is why it is imperative that the shepherds of God's flock not neglect the Word.

Moreover, the local church cannot mature or be protected from its archenemy—the false teacher—without His Word, the bread of God. Therefore, it would be an incalculable loss for the apostles to neglect the preaching of God's Word. To neglect preaching the Word would destroy the church in Jersualem and deny the world the most significant message it could ever hear. The *New English Bible* expresses the apostles' concern well: "It would be a grave mistake for us to neglect the word of God in order to wait at table."

The need to teach God's Word applies to shepherds of every age. John Owen (1616-1683), the distinguished Puritan commentator, recognized the relevance of this principle:

> The same care is still incumbent on the ordinary pastors and elders of the churches, so far as the execution of [charity]

> doth not interfere with their principle work and duty; *from which those who understand it aright can spare but little of their time and strength* (italics added).[1]

The shepherds of God's blood-bought church must be willing to say with the same confidence as the apostles, "It is not [right]...to neglect the teaching of the Word of God to serve tables."

A Clear Focus on the Right Priorities

After their emphatic pronouncement that it was not right to neglect the teaching of God's Word, the apostles declare to the whole church their divinely appointed priorities: "'But we will devote ourselves to prayer, and to the ministry of the word'" (Acts 6:4). Richard N. Longenecker, in *The Expositor's Bible Commentary,* says the word "devote" "connotes a steadfast and single-minded fidelity to a certain course of action."[2] The apostles were on the right track: they were to steadfastly and singlemindedly give themselves to prayer and the ministry of the Word.

I am convinced that Acts 6:4 is one of the most important verses in the New Testament for church shepherds. It enunciates the fundamental priorities of all church shepherds: prayer and the ministry of the Word. Church shepherds are so easily sidetracked. So many good things demand time and energy; there are always many people who need counsel, programs that need administering, and meetings to attend. Thus the shepherds' time for prayer, Bible study, and teaching the Word of God is slighted. A pastor of a small church told me it took him from Monday through Thursday to perform his administrative duties, which left only Friday and part of Saturday in which to prepare a message from the Word of God. My response was to encourage him to read Acts 6 and reorder his priorities.

We must remember that the true priorities of church leaders are always under attack. There will always be too much to do. "Overbusyness" is destroying the lives of many servants of God as well as many churches. Robert and Julia Banks, a leading Australian couple involved in the home church movement, write: "The cult of busyness and activism that infects Christians so much today is one of the greatest barriers to the church becoming what it should be."[3] So church shepherds must radically insist on a schedule that affirms the spiritual priorities of prayer and the ministry of God's Word. The deacons of the church, also, need to fix these priorities firmly in their minds. This is what the apostles were doing in their pronouncement to the congregation.

Prayer

Acts 6:1-4 can be called a success story because the apostles demonstrated that they had learned their lessons from Jesus. What enabled them to so confidently state their priorities? They had been with Jesus. They had seen Him live and minister as a man of prayer and the Word (Mark 1:35-39). Like their Master, they were men of prayer. Prayer had become a major part of their work. They were not building ships for the fishing industry in Galilee; they were building people for God. They were involved in spiritual conflict over the souls of men and women. Therefore, prayer was one of their foremost duties.

The shepherds of God's precious flock must understand that *prayer is the shepherds' work*, and that it requires time and energy. Hudson Taylor, founder of the China Inland Mission, once cautioned, "Do not be so busy with the work of Christ (or anything else) that you have no strength left for praying. True prayer requires strength." William Carey, father of modern missions and missionary to India, has been quoted as saying, "Prayer is my real business! Cobbling shoes is a sideline; it just helps me pay expenses." Prayer is clearly the shepherds' real business. Shepherds would do well to keep the words of James before them in all their pastoral labors: "The effective prayer of a righteous man can accomplish much" (James 5:16).

Much more should be said about the indispensable role that prayer plays in the shepherds' ministry, but space does not permit.

So I will conclude with a stirring challenge and sound counsel from Paul E. Billheimer's inspiring book, *Destined for the Throne:*

> A church without an intelligent, well-organized, and systematic prayer program is simply operating a religious treadmill.... Any church program, no matter how impressive, if it is not supported by an adequate prayer program, is little more than an ecclesiastical treadmill. It is doing little or no damage to Satan's kingdom....
>
> Does anyone imagine that souls are delivered from Satan's bondage by means of human talent, the hypnotic power of human personality, the charm of human magnetism, eloquence, articulateness, or the magic of Madison Avenue techniques? All of these gifts God may use, but alone they are utterly powerless to deliver even one soul from the captivity of sin.[4]

The Word

Alongside the shepherds' priority of prayer is the ministry of the Word—evangelism and teaching of believers. Prayer and the Word must always go together. Our Lord was a mighty man of prayer and the Word. E. M. Bounds, author of many books on prayer, warns of the spiritual weakness of prayerless preachers: "The pulpit of this day is weak in praying. The pride of learning is against the dependent humility of prayer.... Every preacher who does not make prayer a mighty factor in his own life and ministry is weak as a factor in God's work."

Throughout the New Testament, we witness the priority that Christ and His followers place on proclaiming and teaching the Word of God. In Mark 3:14, we read, "And He appointed twelve, that they might be with Him, and that He might send them out to preach." From the start of Christianity, on the day of Pentecost, we read about the principal role of teaching and proclaiming the Word. Peter preached the Word and three thousand people were converted. To a room full of eager listeners, Peter said that Christ had commanded him and his fellow apostles to preach the Word: "'And He ordered us to preach to the people, and solemnly to testify that this is the One...'" (Acts 10:42). If the apostles spent too much time caring for the welfare of widows, their primary mission of spreading the Word to unbelievers and teaching the church would have been seriously hindered. The Word of God had to go forth.

Preaching the Word is no less important to church shepherds today. Note how the late D. Martyn Lloyd-Jones, of Westminster Chapel in London, summarizes this passage:

> Now there the priorities are laid down once and for ever. This is the primary task of the Church, the primary task of the leaders of the Church, the people who are set in this position of authority; and we must not allow anything to deflect us from this, however good the cause, however great the need.[5]

Lloyd-Jones emphasizes that powerful teaching of the Word of God has ignited all the great revivals of Christianity. Likewise, all the decadent eras of Christianity resulted from the loss of Scripture's centrality in the work of God. He writes:

> Is it not clear, as you take a bird's-eye view of Church history, that the decadent periods and eras in the history of the Church have always been those periods when preaching had declined? What is it that always heralds the dawn of a Reformation or of a Revival? It is renewed preaching.... A revival of true preaching has always heralded these great movements in the history of the Church.[6]

J. I. Packer, widely known author and professor at Regent College in Canada, also believes that church renewal will be futile if it is not founded on biblical preaching: "I constantly maintain that if today's quest for renewal is not, along with its other concerns, a quest for true preaching, it will prove shallow and barren."[7]

The major distinguishing characteristic of the New Testament church is the centrality of proclaiming and teaching the

Word of God. So when shepherds neglect the Word of God, they sabotage the work of God. Therefore, the lessons of Acts 6:1-4 must be repeatedly rehearsed, as John R. W. Stott, former Rector of All Souls' Church in London and an honorary chaplain to the queen of England, so aptly states:

> The Church of every generation has to re-learn the lesson of Acts 6. There was nothing wrong with the apostles' zeal for God and his Church. They were busily engaged in a Christlike, compassionate ministry to needy widows. But it was not the ministry to which they, as apostles, had been called. Their vocation was "the ministry of the Word and prayer"; the social care of the widows was the responsibility of others.[8]

Stott goes on to encourage preachers by saying,

> If today's pastors were to take seriously the New Testament emphasis on the priority of preaching and teaching, not only would they find it extremely fulfilling themselves, but also it would undoubtedly have a very wholesome effect on the Church. Instead, tragic to relate, many are essentially administrators, whose symbols of ministry are the office rather than the study, and the telephone rather than the Bible.[9]

The apostles had their priorities straight and were determined to keep them straight. The church prospered spiritually and numerically because of their unwavering commitment.

Let us heed the words of that godly judge of Israel, Samuel, that they might be burned permanently into our hearts and minds in order to guide our spiritual priorities:

> "...far be it from me that I should sin against the Lord by ceasing to pray for you; but I will instruct you in the good and right way" (1 Samuel 12:23).

Chapter 2

Appointing Ministers of Mercy

Now at this time while the disciples were increasing in number, a complaint arose on the part of the Hellenistic Jews against the native Hebrews, because their widows were being overlooked in the daily serving of food.

Acts 6:1

"But select from among you, brethren, seven men of good reputation, full of the Spirit and of wisdom, whom we may put in charge of this task."

Acts 6:3

Acts 2

To open the Book of Acts and read about the extraordinary love and unity among the first Christians is positively exhilarating to the soul. In Acts 2:44,45, we read:

> And all those who had believed were together, and had all things in common; and they began selling their property and possessions, and were sharing them with all, as anyone might have need.

This was a literal fulfillment of our Lord's teaching:

> "Do not be afraid, little flock, for your Father has chosen gladly to give you the kingdom. Sell your possessions and give to charity; make yourselves purses which do not wear out, an unfailing treasure in heaven.... For where your treasure is, there will your heart be also" (Luke 12:32-34).

ACTS 4

In Acts 4, we discover that these Christians continued their lavish display of love and care for one another. Their care for the needy became so extensive that money and goods had to be brought directly to the apostles for effective distribution. Theirs was not a Sunday-morning-only Christianity. It was what life together in the visible, Spirit-indwelt community of the risen Lord is to be like. It was the kind of self-sacrificing love that Jesus Christ expects His people to demonstrate.

> And the congregation of those who believed were of one heart and soul; and not one of them claimed that anything belonging to him was his own; but all things were common property to them.... For there was not a needy person among them, for all who were owners of land or houses would sell them and bring the proceeds of the sales, and lay them at the apostles' feet; and they would be distributed to each, as any had need (Acts 4:32,34,35).

Deeply touched by this passage, the French reformer, John Calvin (1509-1564), dramatically contrasts the attitude of these first Jewish Christians with the self-seeking behavior of many Christians in his day. (His words, we have to admit, also apply to our own day.) Calvin writes:

> Now we must have hearts that are harder than iron if

> we are not moved by the reading of this narrative. In those days the believers gave abundantly of what was their own; we in our day are content not just jealously to retain what we possess, but callously to rob others.... They sold their own possessions in those days; in our day it is the lust to purchase that reigns supreme. At that time love made each man's own possessions common property for those in need; in our day such is the inhumanity of many, that they begrudge to the poor a common dwelling upon earth....[1]

What motivated these first Christians to care for one another to this extent? Calvin is right when he says, "...love made each man's own possessions common property for those in need." Jesus commanded His disciples to love one another with the same kind of self-sacrificing love He had shown them: "This is My commandment, that you love one another, just as I have loved you. Greater love has no one than this, that one lay down his life for his friends" (John 15:12,13). And He did just that. In the supreme act of love, He gave up His life for them and for us. Therefore, says the renowned Presbyterian theologian, B. B. Warfield (1851-1921), "Self-sacrificing love is thus made the essence of the Christian life."[2]

Acts 6

In Acts 6, we again see evidence of the believers' remarkable love for one another. The continuous outpouring of love and service of the church in Jerusalem was evident on a daily basis through its efforts to feed its poor widows:

> Now at this time while the disciples were increasing in number, a complaint arose on the part of the Hellenistic Jews against the native Hebrews, because their widows were being overlooked in the daily serving of food (Acts 6:1).

Feeding the Christian widows was an enormous job that demanded considerable time, effort, and money. This was not token giving, nor was it Christmastime or tax season. This was authentic, Spirit-filled, love-filled Christianity in action—every day of the year.

A Warning to Christians Today

This extravagant display of generosity, however, could not have existed if these Christians were worried about maintaining their standard of living or if the church at Jerusalem had spent all of its money on buildings or salaries. Nothing so effectively dulls the senses of Christians to the needs of hurting people as love for earthly possessions. D. Martyn Lloyd- Jones writes:

> These earthly treasures are so powerful that they grip the entire personality. They grip a man's heart, his mind and his will; they tend to affect his spirit, his soul and his whole being. Whatever realm of life we may be looking at, or thinking about, we shall find these things are there. Everyone is affected by them; they are a terrible danger.[3]

A Brazilian bishop and compassionate advocate of the poor confesses:

> I used to think, when I was a child, that Christ might have been exaggerating when he warned about the dangers of wealth. Today I know better. I know how very hard it is to be rich and still keep the milk of human kindness. Money has a dangerous way of putting scales on one's eyes, a dangerous way of freezing people's hands, eyes, lips and hearts.[4]

Because of the overwhelmingly magnetic power that material possessions have to turn us away from godly compassion and eternal values, our Lord gave stern warnings against the dangers of greed: "'Beware, and be on your guard against every form of greed; for not even when one has an abundance does his life consist of his possessions'" (Luke 12:15). Let us heed our Lord's warning, lest our hands, eyes, lips and hearts become frozen so that we cannot share with those who suffer need.

The Ministers of Word and Deed

The Christians' marvelous display of love and care was threatened, however, by discriminating practices in the distribution of funds to the Hellenistic widows. Courageously, the apostles assumed full responsibility for the problem. Ultimately the injustice was their fault, since they were responsible for the pastoral oversight of the congregation. They recognized that they could no longer give the time and attention required to the task of administering the church's funds to the needy. Things could not continue as they had. The apostles were busy, and as the church increased in size and complexity, so did their work load. Moreover, their primary duties as shepherds were to be prayer and the teaching of the Word, not widows' relief. Something had to be done to relieve their expanding work load.

As a body of humble, godly pastors, they consulted with one another and their Lord about this problem. After agreeing on a proposed solution, Luke records that, "the twelve summoned the congregation of the disciples." After the congregation assembled, the apostles presented a plan for solving the problem. "'But select from among you, brethren'" they said, "'seven men of good reputation, full of the Spirit and of wisdom, whom we may put in charge of this task.'"

The apostles' plan called for the formation of a body of seven men to whom they could hand over responsibility for the widows' care. They asked the people to select the men, but because of the apostles' intimate knowledge of the demanding task, they laid down qualifications to guide the congregation in the selection process. Not just any Christian could do the job. The apostles knew that the task demanded skilled men of high moral character who could be trusted to fulfill the responsibilities with integrity and ability. The wrong men could create worse problems and frustrate the apostles even more than the existing situation.

By solving the problem in this way, the apostles formed a new body of church officials. The two major categories of officials in the church at Jerusalem were the apostles and the Seven. The apostles were to devote themselves to prayer and to the proclamation of the Word. Hence, their work was primarily a verbal ministry. The newly appointed officials were to give themselves to a ministry of deeds—to provide loving service to needy brothers and sisters in Christ.

In Scripture these two broad classifications of ministry are described as "word" and "deed" (Romans 15:18; Colossians 3:17). In Acts 6, Luke defines these classifications as the "ministry of the Word" (v. 4) and the "serving of food" (v. 2). Peter defines them as speaking and serving, which is the same as word and deed. He writes, "Whoever speaks, let him speak, as it were, the utterances of God; whoever serves, let him do so as by the strength which God supplies; so that in all things God may be glorified through Jesus Christ..." (1 Peter 4:11). In both cases, speaking or serving, God is the source of power, the One who receives glory from what is done.

Some people are strong in both word and deed. For example, Scripture says that Moses and Jesus were "mighty in deed and word" (Luke 24:19; Acts 7:22). But most of us are stronger in one area than the other (although we must not neglect our weaker area of spiritual development). We must understand that the work of Jesus Christ demands both kinds of people. Both are essential to the work of God.

Those who are strong in word tend to be teachers, preachers, writers, counselors, shepherds, or students. For example, Apollos was mighty in the Word. Luke describes Apollos this way:

> ...an eloquent man, came to Ephesus, and he was mighty in the Scriptures. This man had been instructed in the way of the Lord; and being fervent in spirit, he was speaking and

> teaching accurately the things concerning Jesus...for he powerfully refuted the Jews in public, demonstrating by the Scripture that Jesus was the Christ (Acts 18:24*b*,25*a*,28).

People who are strong in deeds, on the other hand, tend to be administrators, organizers, doers, helpers, supporters, builders, ministers of mercy, and givers. Stephanas and his family, Onesiphorus, Phoebe, Onesimus, and the women who contributed to our Lord's ministry were all recognized in the New Testament for their loving service to others, not their speaking ministry (1 Corinthians 16:15; 2 Timothy 1:16-18; Romans 16:1; Philemon 10-13; Luke 8:3). Of Onesiphorus, Paul writes, "...when he was in Rome, he eagerly searched for me, and found me—the Lord grant to him to find mercy from the Lord on that day—and you know very well what services [*diakoneō*] he rendered at Ephesus" (2 Timothy 1:17,18).

The Seven, as a group, were appointed to a ministry of deeds, although, at least two of them were also mighty in word. No matter which gifts or other interests the individual men had, as a group they were the church's administrators of charitable welfare. This in no way suggests, however, that only the Seven (or deacons today) had the responsibility to care for the needy.

When the apostles said, "But we will devote ourselves to prayer, and to the ministry of the word," they didn't mean they would exclusively spend their time teaching and never again help needy people. The apostles faced the problem that their charitable work was hindering them from doing the primary job of proclaiming Christ. Although their primary duties are to teach and govern, they are to be concerned for the needy, too. In Galatians 2:10, we see the apostles' concern for the poor when they ask Paul "to remember the poor." Paul, who God appointed to be a preacher, an apostle, and a teacher (1 Timothy 2:7), responded, "...the very thing I also was eager to do." (See also Acts 24:17; 2 Corinthians 8,9.)

Paul also emphasizes the importance of caring for the poor in his instruction to the Ephesian elders:

> "You yourselves know that these hands ministered to my

> own needs and to the men who were with me. In everything I showed you that by working hard in this manner you must help the weak and remember the words of the Lord Jesus, that He Himself said, 'It is more blessed to give than to receive'" (Acts 20:34,35, cf. Acts 11:29,30).

So it is not only the deacons' responsibility to help the needy, although they are the official church coordinators of benevolence. Every Christian—shepherd, apostle, teacher—is to be concerned about helping the needy.

UNDERSTANDING THE SEVEN'S TASK

If any organization is to maintain integrity and effectiveness, good management of funds and resources is essential.

Some Christians seem to equate disorganization with spirituality, but just the opposite is true. Disorganization and mismanagement always significantly multiplies problems and frustrate people. A newspaper reported that the Director of the General Accounting Office, Charles Bowsher, informed the Congress of the United States that 150 billion dollars or more of taxpayers' money would be wasted in 1992 by mismanagement: "Bowsher said the multibillion-dollar scandals...were likely to be followed by billions more in fraud, waste and abuse for a common reason: lousy management."[5]

Mismanagement and disorganization ruins families, businesses, governments, and churches. It is the product of the polluted soil of greed, laziness, carelessness, lovelessness, and selfishness. It is not from God. Therefore the family of God should not be mismanaged. God should receive our best effort, energy, and skill. The entire account of Acts 6 is a sterling example of good organization and loving care for the people of God.

The task the apostles gave to the Seven was specific. Its nature is partially described as "the daily serving" (Acts 6:1) and "to serve tables" (v. 2). The Greek word for *tables, trapeza*, is often used figuratively to mean food or meals (Acts 16:34). But the term *tables* is also used figuratively for finances, a money table, or a bank (Luke 19:23). For example, the *Good News Bible* translates Acts 6:2 this way: "'It is not right for us to neglect the preaching of God's word in order to handle finances.'" It also renders the end of Acts 6:1 as "daily distribution of funds." In *The New Testament in Modern English*, J. B. Phillips gives his rendering of verse 2: "'It is not right that we should have to neglect preaching the Word of God in order to look after the accounts.'"

If *tables* here means money tables, then the Seven were to distribute money for food daily to the widows and keep careful accounts of their expenditures. If not, the Seven were to administer communal meals for these widows, which of course would involve money and accounting. It is difficult to be certain, but Acts 4:34,35 suggests that we are to understand *tables* to mean money tables where money is distributed and collected.

In detail, the Seven were:

(1) to collect money and goods contributed to the needy (Acts 4:34,35,37; 5:2);

(2) to distribute the money or goods to the needy (Acts 4:35);

(3) to ensure that the church justly and fairly distributed the money; and

(4) to coordinate the church's overall charitable services to the needy.

The Seven, in other words, were the church's official ministers of mercy. Through them the church's charitable activities were effectively centralized. They represented the church's corporate response to its needy widows. As we all know, welfare activities can be easily abused by both giver and receiver. But the Seven, acting as the church's official administrators of charity, could ensure that the church's widows and other needy members would receive fair and highly efficient service.

Finally, the primary focus of the Seven's task was to assist the needy of the Christian community, not all the poor of Jerusalem (Acts 2:44,45; 4:32-37; 6:1). It was imperative that the new community of the risen Savior care for its needy. Among the Jews in Jerusalem, as the German scholar, Joachim Jeremias, reveals in his book, *Jerusalem in the Time of Jesus*, groups and individuals provided assistance for needy fellow citizens in Jerusalem.[6] In fact, some Jewish Christian widows may have been cut off from such help because of their newfound faith. So the Christians could do no less in the way of relief for their own.

The church in Jerusalem could have no credible witness to its unbelieving Jewish neighbors if it did not care for its widows.

That doesn't mean the Christians were to help no one outside their circle. Christians, as Scripture teaches, are to show mercy and love to all needy people (Luke 10:37; 1 Thessalonians 3:12). But the Seven's first duty, *as the church's official body of mercy ministers,* was to manage relief efforts for the church's suffering members.

From Luke's point of view, the gospel's advancement was intimately connected with solving the poor widows' problems. The gospel had to go forward to the ends of the earth, but at the same time needy members of the Christian community had to be supported or the gospel message would lose credibility. Immediately after Luke records the appointment of the Seven to care for poor widows, he writes, "And the word of God kept on spreading; and the number of the disciples continued to increase greatly in Jerusalem..." (Acts 6:7).

Chapter 3

Official Public Recognition

And the statement found approval with the whole congregation; and they chose Stephen, a man full of faith and of the Holy Spirit, and Philip, Prochorus, Nicanor, Timon, Parmenas and Nicolas, a proselyte from Antioch. And these they brought before the apostles; and after praying, they laid their hands on them.

Acts 6:5,6

The Apostles Solicit Congregational Involvement

The conflict between the Hellenistic and Hebrew Jews in Jerusalem could have turned into an ugly church division that lasted for decades. Instead, acting in humble accord with one another and the congregation, the apostles peacefully resolved the highly explosive situation. Acts 6 magnificently illustrates that the apostles had learned (after numerous failures of fighting among themselves for name and position) the distinctive principles of Christlike leadership (Matthew 23:1-12; Mark 9:30-35; 10:35-45; Luke 22:24-27). They had learned to be humble and loving shepherds.

As a wise pastoral body, the Twelve knew the importance of

involving the entire congregation in solving this problem. The apostles could have acted without the whole congregation, but they didn't, for several key reasons.

First, the apostles knew that they needed to treat the congregation as brothers and sisters in Christ who were indwelt by the Holy Spirit of God. The apostles were not the people's priestly clerics, and the people were not their disciples.

Second, the apostles knew that the money belonged to the people, and the widows were the people's responsibility. So the problem was everyone's problem. The congregation had to share in the responsibility of planning and administering its charitable business.

Third, the apostles sought to protect themselves from potential, sinister charges regarding money and power. The apostles were all Hebrews, not Hellenistic Jews. According to the apostles' plan, the congregation could pick administrators who represented them more equitably. In this way, the apostles could not be accused of partiality.

This was important because, in all likelihood, even the apostles were financially supported by the congregation. If the apostles picked their own men to administer the relief efforts, people could accuse the apostles of controlling the money. The apostles, however, were not concerned about money and control. They were not greedy. Their decision to delegate the responsibility of handling the church's charitable funds to others should be an example to Christian leaders today who think they must control everything, especially the money.

The Congregation Selects Seven Men

The congregation responded to the apostles' plan with unanimous approval: "And the statement found approval with the whole congregation." The congregation immediately proceeded to choose seven men. Luke writes, "They chose Stephen, a man full of faith and of the Holy Spirit, and Philip, Prochorus, Nicanor, Timon, Parmenas and Nicolas, a proselyte from Antioch."

OFFICIAL PUBLIC RECOGNITION

Exactly how the congregation in Jerusalem selected seven of its men is not recorded. It would not have been difficult for the congregation to organize itself for such a selection, for they had ample examples to follow. When feeding massive numbers of people, for instance, our Lord quickly organized them into manageable groups "of hundreds and of fifties" for orderly distribution (Mark 6:40). From its earliest days, the nation of Israel was organized into precisely defined, manageable groups for communication, war, service, and travel (Exodus 13:18; 18:13- 27; 36:6; Numbers 2:2ff; 7:2; 1 Kings 4:7). Congregational decisions and operations were conducted primarily through representatives or heads of clans and towns (Compare Leviticus 4:13 with 4:15; Exodus 3:15,16; compare Exodus 4:29 with 4:31; Exodus 19:7,8; Deuteronomy 21:1,2,6-9). So it is quite possible that the congregation in Jerusalem was already organized into similar manageable units. Such organization would enable issues to be decided and information to be passed along quickly (Acts 12:12,17; Acts 15:4,6,22; 21:17,18).

THE SEVEN RECEIVE THE APOSTLES' APPROVAL

After selecting the Seven, the congregation presented them to the apostles for official approval. Rather than immediately sending the Seven out to work, the congregation brought them to the apostles, who commissioned them in an official and public way, by the laying on of hands and prayer.[1]

It is only natural that the apostles would be responsible for placing the Seven in charge of the church's money and ministries to the needy. Indeed, the apostles' proposed plan, as outlined in verse 3, states that the apostles would "put in charge of this task" those selected by the congregation:

> "But select from among you, brethren, seven men of good reputation, full of the Spirit and of wisdom, whom *we may put in charge of this task*" (italics added).

The subject of the Greek verb that means "put in charge" (first person plural) is the twelve apostles. The subject of the Greek verb that means "select" (second person plural) is the "congregation of the disciples." The Greek verb that means "put in charge," *kathistēmi*, is often used to express appointment to an official position, such as the appointment of a judge or governor (Acts 7:10). It can also express appointment in an unofficial sense. Either way, the verb indicates a sense of authority, as R. J. Knowling in *The Expositor's Greek Testament* states: "The verb implies at all events an exercise of authority."[2]

The apostles could officially place the Seven in charge of helping the church's needy and distributing church finances because they had the authority, as Christ's chosen apostles, to do so (Ephesians 2:19,20). Therefore, it is best to understand that the congregation chose the seven men and the apostles officially installed them.

The Laying on of Hands

When the apostles installed the Seven, Scripture says, "they laid their hands on them" (Acts 6:6). This is the first recorded example of the laying on of hands in the Christian community. The imposition of hands is used for various reasons in the Bible, but as James Orr, a well-known Scottish apologist for orthodox Christianity at the turn of the century, writes, "The primary idea seems to be that of conveyance or transference (cf. Leviticus 16:21) but, conjoined with this, in certain instances are the ideas of identification and of devotion to God."[3]

Looking first at Old Testament examples, we note that the laying on of hands was used to:

- convey blessing (Genesis 48:14)
- identify with a sacrifice to God (Leviticus 1:4)
- transfer sin (Leviticus 16:21)
- transfer defilement (Leviticus 24:14)
- identify man's actions with God's (2 Kings 13:16)

- set people apart, such as in conveying a special commission, responsibility, or authority (Numbers 8:10,14; 27:15-23; Deuteronomy 34:9)

In the New Testament, the laying on of hands was used to:

- convey blessing (Matthew 19:15; Mark 10:16)
- convey the Holy Spirit's healing power (Mark 6:5; 8:23,25; 16:18; Luke 4:40; 13:13; Acts 9:12; 19:11; 28:8)
- convey the Holy Spirit to certain believers through the apostles' hands (Acts 8:17-19; 19:6)
- convey healing and the Holy Spirit to Paul through Ananias' hands (Acts 9:17)
- convey a spiritual gift to Timothy through Paul's hands (2 Timothy 1:6)
- set apart or place in office (Acts 6:6; 13:3; 1 Timothy 4:14; 5:22)

The New Testament contains no normative regulations for the laying on of hands. It is not a prescribed practice such as baptism or the Lord's Supper, nor is it restricted to a particular person or group in the church (Acts 9:12; 13:3). So the precise significance of the laying on of hands is difficult to determine at times. We do know that the imposition of hands, like fasting, was practiced by the first Christians because it was useful and a blessing to all. Christians are free, then, to use the laying on of hands if they desire, or to refrain from its practice if it leads to misunderstanding.

Because of confusion or superstition surrounding the laying on of hands, many churches today avoid its use entirely. That is unfortunate because the laying on of hands can be a meaningful public act.

In light of this background, it seems reasonable to assume that the imposition of hands in Acts 6 visually expressed the apostles' blessing, commissioned the Seven to a special task (Numbers 27:22,23), and transferred the authority to do the job.

OFFICIAL PUBLIC RECOGNITION

Because of the Seven's responsible task of handling large sums of money (Acts 4:34-37) and the growing tensions between the Hellenistic Jews and Hebrews, the apostles knew that the situation demanded an official, public act of appointment.

The laying on of hands in Acts 6, however, did not install the Seven to higher ministerial positions (priest or minister), nor did it make the Seven successors to the apostles. It was not ordination that authorized them to preach and administer the sacraments. It did not convey grace or the Holy Spirit, for the Seven were already filled with the Holy Spirit. Rather, *the laying on of hands commissioned the Seven to serve the needy.* How different this is from customary traditions of laying hands only on the highest clergy!

THE IMPORTANCE OF THE SEVEN'S TASK

The laying on of hands, along with the early appearance of this account in Acts, indicates the significance and necessity of the Seven's task. Some people might find it hard to believe that appointing men to care for poor widows and handle money would require the laying on of the apostles' hands. Those who don't understand why the apostles took this matter so seriously don't understand how important the care of the poor is in God's eyes. As the Scripture says, "This is pure and undefiled religion in the sight of our God and Father, to visit orphans and widows in their distress..." (James 1:27*a*).

The saintly, Scottish revivalist and pastor Robert Murray McCheyne (1813-1843) understood the importance of giving to the poor and used the strongest possible words to teach his congregation in Dundee, Scotland, the necessity of giving to needy people. Prayerfully read the following closing words of his sermon on Acts 20:35, "It is more blessed to give than to receive":

> I fear there are some Christians among you to whom Christ cannot say ["Well done, good and faithful servant"].

> Your haughty dwelling raises amidst of thousands who have scarce a fire to warm themselves at, and have but little clothing to keep out the biting frost; and yet you never darkened their door. You heave a sigh, perhaps, at a distance; but you do not visit them. Ah! my dear friends! I am concerned for the poor, but more for you. I know not what Christ will say to you in the great day. You seem to be Christians, and yet you care not for his poor. Oh, what a change will pass upon you as you enter the gates of heaven! You will be saved, but that will be all. There will be no abundant entrance for you: 'He that soweth sparingly shall reap also sparingly'.
>
> I fear there are many hearing me who may know well that they are not Christians, because they do not love to give. To give largely and liberally, not grudging at all, requires a new heart; an old heart would rather part with its life-blood than its money. Oh, my friends! enjoy your money; make the most of it; give none away; enjoy it quickly, for I can tell you, you will be beggars throughout eternity.[4]

John Owen reminds us that many of the first Christians were poor: "Many of them who first received it were of the state and condition, as the Scripture everywhere testifieth: 'The poor are evangelized,' Matt. 11:5; 'God hath chosen the poor,' James 2:5."[5] Therefore, care for the poor and needy, Owen adds, was "one of the most eminent graces and duties of the church in those days."[6] We must never, he cautions, treat flippantly this important responsibility to the poor and disadvantaged:

> ...if all churches, and all the members of them, would wisely consider how eminent is this grace, how excellent is this duty, of making provision for the poor,—how much the glory of Christ and honour of the gospel are concerned herein; for whereas, for the most part, it is looked on as an ordinary work, to be performed transiently and cursorily,

scarce deserving any of the time which is allotted unto the church's public service and duties, it is indeed one of the most eminent duties of Christian societies...."[7]

Biblical commentator William Barclay relates an old legend that beautifully illustrates the value of the poor and the importance of caring for them:

> In the days of the terrible Decian persecution in Rome, the Roman authorities broke into a Christian Church. They were out to loot the treasures which they believed the Church to possess. The Roman prefect demanded from Laurentius, the deacon: "Show me your treasures at once." Laurentius pointed at the widows and orphans who were being supplied, "These," he said, "are the treasures of the Church."[8]

No wonder the Seven were commissioned for their work through the laying on of hands! Thereby they were given official status to handle the important work of caring for the church's needy. The Seven formed a distinct body of officials who were separate from the apostles. They were not equal with the apostles, nor were they junior apostles or shepherds in training. They did not become assistants to the apostles. The Seven formed a separate but complementary ministry to that of the apostles.

Why the Need for Official Servants

First Peter 4:10 affirms that every Christian has a spiritual gift from God that is to be used in serving others: "As each one has received a special gift, employ it in serving one another, as good stewards of the manifold grace of God." If all Christians are to be servants, why then were designated, official servants needed to minister to the needy in the Jerusalem church?

Acts 6 demonstrates that certain service tasks require people who have select skills and proven moral character. Administering large amounts of charitable funds, for instance, requires people who possess irreproachable character, godly wisdom, and administrative skills. The sad truth is, some Christians steal. For these Christians it is too great a temptation to hold large amounts of money. Therefore, qualified, official servants are needed to perform these duties.

Furthermore, the Bible warns that the poor, especially widows, are vulnerable to exploitation. Jesus said to beware of the scribes "who devour widows' houses" (Luke 20:47). Likewise, religious swindlers abound, preying on widows and the elderly. No church should expose people who need the most protection and care to unknown or unstable people. So, select servants will always be needed to officially represent the local church in delicate matters of trust and to coordinate the church's charity.

A Final Warning

Acts 6 is not a list of regulations and rules, so it should not be interpreted as a strict blueprint to be followed in every detail. For example, the apostles asked that seven men must be chosen. The question arises, then, if that means every church must have seven deacons. Some Christians of the second, third, and fourth centuries believed this and allowed only seven deacons per city. The council of Neo-Caesarea in the year A.D. 315 stated in one of its canons that the number of deacons in a city must be seven.

The number seven, however, met the unique needs of the church at Jerusalem, as did the other detailed procedures of the apostles' plan. Thus a local church today has flexibility in how its deacons are chosen, how many are selected, and what they specifically are to do. As long as the deacons enable the shepherds of the church to carry out their primary duties, and as long as the deacons minister to the congregation's welfare needs, they are doing their job.

Chapter 4

Acts 6: The Prototype for Deacons

> **Inasmuch as many have undertaken to compile an account of the things accomplished among us, just as those who from the beginning were eyewitnesses and servants of the word have handed them down to us, it seemed fitting for me as well, having investigated everything carefully from the beginning, to write it out for you in consecutive order, most excellent Theophilus; so that you might know the exact truth about the things you have been taught.**
>
> **Luke 1:1-4**

Can we legitimately assume that the Seven in Acts 6 are the forerunners to the later deacons? In the two passages in which Paul mentions deacons, Philippians 1:1 and 1 Timothy 3:8-13, he offers no explanation of the deacons' origin or of their duties. His readers, of course, already knew the deacons' origin and responsibilities. But where do Christians today find such an explanation?

Although Luke does not state that the seven men mentioned in Acts 6 were the first deacons, many commentators since the middle of the second century have assumed that the Seven were the first deacons. Irenaeus (A.D. c.130-c.200), bishop of Lyons in

Gaul (modern France), was the first writer to clearly identify the Seven as "deacons."[1]

Objections to the Seven as the Prototype of Deacons

Other biblical commentators, however, dismiss the idea that Acts 6 has anything to do with deacons. Gordon Fee, professor of New Testament at Regent College in Vancouver, Canada, claims:

> An appeal to Acts 6:1-6 is of no value, since those men are not called deacons. In fact they are clearly ministers of the Word among Greek-speaking Jews, who eventually accrue the title "the Seven" (Acts 21:8), which distinguishes them in a way similar to "the Twelve."[2]

Although Luke does not state explicitly that the Seven were the first deacons, the content of Luke's account, in which the apostles officially appointing a body of men to administer church funds to the needy, leads many people to conclude that there is a definite connection. Surely Acts 6 should not be brushed aside. As we will see, Dr. Fee's objections, which represent the most common objections, are misleading and unsound.

The Missing Word

It is a mistake to conclude that because the Seven are not actually called *deacons*, there is no connection between the Seven mentioned in Acts and the deacons mentioned in Paul's epistles. The fact that Luke does not state that the Seven are deacons is consistent with his style of historical reporting in both the Gospel of Luke and the Acts of the Apostles.

Luke is very accurate in writing history, particularly in his use of terminology for persons and places. Concerning Luke's ability as a historian, the late F. F. Bruce, one of the most prolific and distinguished commentators of the twentieth century, quotes the distinguished historian Eduard Meyer's evaluation of Luke:

> Eduard Meyer, the greatest twentieth-century historian of classical antiquity, considered Luke the one great historian who joins the last of the genuinely Greek historians, Polybius, to the greatest of Christian historians, Eusebius. Luke's work, he reckoned, "in spite of its more restricted content, bears the same character as those of the great historians, of a Polybius, a Livy, and many others."[3]

When Luke refers to Philip in Acts 21:8, he identifies him as an evangelist and "one of the seven," but does not identify him as a deacon. The reason for this identification is that Luke accurately represents the historical situation and terminology used at the time of the events of Acts 6. Undoubtedly the office-title *deacon*, (Greek, *diakonos*, which means "servant"), was not used at that time in the church's development. Even though Luke knew that people were called deacons in his day, he did not give in to the temptation of making the history of Acts fit later church development and terminology. In other words, he did not write anachronistically. Thus "the record of Acts," Bruce states, "is true to its 'dramatic' date, i.e., to the date of the events and developments which it relates."[4]

We might think that Luke should have at least commented on the connection between the Seven and the deacons, but again that was not his method of historical writing. For example, Luke does not tell us the position that our Lord's half brother, James, held in the church, although James is a predominant figure in the Jerusalem church and was most likely an apostle (Galatians 1:19). Luke never clearly states that Paul—the great apostle to the Gentiles—was an apostle, although his apostleship is evident in Acts. (The statement in Acts 14:4 about Paul's apostleship is somewhat ambiguous.[5])

Luke records momentous events during the beginning years

of Christianity without adding any special comments (Acts 8:5-19; 10:1-48; 13:1-4). He does not match theological solutions or explanations with difficult-to-understand events or practices (Acts 8:14-17; 19:1-7,12; 21:23-26). Likewise, in Acts 6, Luke records no special name or title for this group of men.

A man eminently qualified to evaluate Luke's historical accuracy and style is Sir William Ramsay (1851-1939), who is known for his brilliant, pioneer archeological and historical research on Acts. Ramsay writes:

> It is rare to find a narrative so simple and so little forced as that of *Acts*. It is a mere uncoloured recital of the important facts in the briefest possible terms. The narrator's individuality and his personal feelings and preferences are almost wholly suppressed.... It would be difficult in the whole range of literature to find a work where there is less attempt at pointing a moral or drawing a lesson from the facts. The narrator is persuaded that the facts themselves in their barest form are a perfect lesson and a complete instruction, and he feels that it would be an impertinence and even an impiety to intrude his individual views into the narrative.[6]

Dr. David Gooding, former professor of Greek at Queen's University, Belfast, Ireland, and an expert on the Greek Old Testament, the *Septuagint*, also comments on Luke's style of historical reporting: "Luke...has added the barest minimum of interpretative comment beyond his record of the facts. He has not even invented titles for his sections."[7] Therefore, the fact that Luke does not refer to the Seven as deacons or explain the relationship of the Seven to the later deacons is not surprising. His account speaks for itself.

Missing Word, But Not Missing Concept

Although the word *diakonos*, the Greek word for *deacon,* does not appear in Acts 6, the concept of an official body of servants who lovingly serve others does appear. Furthermore, although *diakonos* does not appear, its corresponding noun, *diakonia*, and verb, *diakoneō,* do. The noun and verb are used to describe the congregation's daily work of providing material help for needy widows.

• "...their widows were being overlooked in the daily *serving* [*diakonia*] of food" (Acts 6:1*b*; italics added).

• "'It is not desirable for us to neglect the word of God in order *to serve* [*diakoneō*] tables'" (Acts 6:2*b*;italics added).

Both the noun *diakonia* and verb *diakoneō* are used in the New Testament, not only in the sense of general service but in the narrower, even technical, sense of attending to people's bodily sufferings and material needs. Such is the case in Acts 6.[8]

The word *diakonos* is plainly used three times in the New Testament to refer to the holder of a specific office (Philippians 1:1; 1 Timothy 3:8,12). It is quite likely that the official title *diakonos* corresponds to the specialized use of its related noun and verb: *diakonia* and *diakoneō*. Professor Charles E. B. Cranfield, emeritus professor of theology, University of Durham, England and author of the massive, two-volume commentary on Romans in the *International Critical Commentary* series, succinctly expresses this linguistic connection:

> We have now seen that there is in the New Testament a specialized technical use of *diakonein* and *diakonia* to denote the practical service of those who are specially needy 'in body, or estate', and that it is highly probable that the specialized technical use of *diakonos* also has the same reference.[9]

Therefore, since an office in the church called *diakonos* is concerned with the physical needs of the people (1 Timothy 3:8-13) and since an official body of men was appointed to help meet (*diakoneō*) the physical needs of the poor (Acts 6:1-6), we cannot but assume there is a connection between the two groups. The inclination to associate the church officers called "servants" (*diakonoi*) in 1 Timothy 3 with those whom the apostles appointed to "serve tables" (*diakoneō*) in Acts 6 is quite natural. At the very least, the similarities should not be ignored.

If the apostles had appointed a body of men to "oversee" the spiritual life of the church so that they could travel, and if in the epistles there was a group called "overseers," certainly we would assume that a connection existed between the two groups. In recording the story found in Acts 6, what else could Luke have thought but that people would associate the Seven with deacons? That is precisely the conclusion of many Bible students during the past two thousand years.

In a sense, we should expect the Book of Acts to help us identify the deacons described in Paul's epistles. The Book of Acts is, in the words of F. F. Bruce, "the second volume to a *History of Christian Origins*."[10] The diaconate is a distinctly Christian institution. People would want to know its origin. Furthermore, the Book of Acts is intended to provide vital background history concerning Paul's teaching and personal practices. For instance, how else would we know that Paul appointed elders in many of the churches he had established? (See Acts 14:23 and 20:17.) We wouldn't. We need to read Acts and Paul's letters together. The Bible is meant to be its best interpreter because the Holy Spirit of God divinely designed the whole of Scripture (2 Timothy 3:16,17).

The Personal Ministries of Stephen and Philip

Dr. Fee's second objection to Acts 6 having any relationship to deacons is that the Seven were "ministers of the Word among Greek-speaking Jews." In the same way, Professor Hermann Wolfgang Beyer, in his massive study on the Greek terms for *service*, writes, "It is to be noted, however, that the seven are set alongside the Twelve as representatives of the Hellenists, and that they take their place with the evangelists and apostles in disputing, preaching and baptizing. This fact shows that the origin of the diaconate is not to be found in Ac. 6."[11]

Neither of these men can accept that such gifted men of the Word could have been deacons or prototype deacons. However, the fact that at least two of the seven (Stephen and Philip) were "ministers of the Word among Greek-speaking Jews" must not obscure *the undeniable truth that these giants of the Word became overseers of relief efforts*. That cannot be disputed, nor should it be ignored.

We must understand, however, that there is a difference between the personal gifts of Stephen and Philip—teaching, evangelism, working miracles—and the special task to which they were appointed, which was administrating the church's charity for the poor. However, there is no incongruity between being a deacon and also being a competent teacher of the Word. Furthermore, we do not know of any official responsibilities that Stephen or Philip held at this time. They were not burdened with the overall pastoral oversight and teaching of the whole church as the apostles were. Only later, after Philip leaves Jerusalem, does he give his full time to preaching the Word to the lost (Acts 8:4-40). At the time of Acts 6, Philip and Stephen could, and did, serve as officers of charitable relief and at the same time teach.

The same is true in churches today. Gifted teachers with earned theological degrees may also serve as deacons. They may teach a Sunday school class or a Bible study in the church, but they do not desire to assume the full pastoral responsibilities of the church. They may hold an office related to serving tables and also teach because of their God-given gift of teaching. We must be cautious not to impose our ideas of deacons and church structure on the New Testament, for it gives us a great deal of latitude in these areas.

Another common error is to think that, because Stephen and Philip had a preaching ministry, part of a deacon's work is to preach and evangelize. Michael Green, professor at Regent College in Vancouver, Canada, writes:

> It is difficult to decide whether Luke thinks of the Seven of Acts 6 as the first Christian deacons. It would be very helpful if so; for it would tell us...that their functions, besides being financial and administrative, involved preaching and disputing with the Jews, evangelism and the performance of wonders and miracles.[12]

This is not true, however. Because Philip baptized people (Acts 8) does not mean that all deacons must baptize. Philip's baptizing of new converts was related to his evangelistic efforts, which he carried out after leaving Jerusalem where he served the church's widows for a certain period of time. The Seven were not chosen by the congregation and appointed by the apostles to teach. Rather, the Seven were commissioned as an official body of servants to the specific task of providing relief to the needy. By virtue of their God-given gifts some of them also taught.

A New Organizational Structure

It is essential at this point that we not overlook the historical fact that the apostles created *a new organizational structure in Jerusalem in order to address a critical, persistent issue: care for the needy*. Prior to the writing of Acts 6, only the twelve apostles held any recognizable office of authority (Acts 1:25). But now, two distinct groups become evident. The new group, an officially authorized body, is appointed to collect and distribute the church's alms to the poor.[13]

There are enough similarities between Acts 6 and the completion of the apostolate in Acts 1 to suggest that the selection of the Seven established a new office in the church. (Read Acts 1:12-26.) In the same way the apostles are named in Acts 1:13,26, the Seven are named in Acts 6:5. Like the Twelve, the Seven have to meet specific qualifications before serving (Acts 1:21,22). Both groups have been appointed to clearly designated tasks. Finally, the laying on of the apostles' hands indicates authorization to serve in an official capacity. Therefore, this was not just volunteer work that was open to everyone in the community. It was an official position, open at that time to only seven men, for the purpose of collecting and distributing the church's money to its needy members.

Luke does not record what became of this official position in the Jerusalem church after persecution scattered many of the Hellenistic Jews (Acts 8). For that matter, Luke never again mentions the sharing of community goods, which he has done three times in the first six chapters of Acts. Such information gaps are the norm throughout the Book of Acts. However, there are no grounds to assume that the institution of the Seven soon disappeared because it was only meant to be a temporary solution to the special circumstances in Jerusalem. Although one theologian says, "Their office was unique and was not continued in the Church,"[14] the needy and the widows surely did not disappear from the church. They still required care.

A Good Model to Follow

No matter what happened to the Seven or to their position in the church at Jerusalem as a result of persecution, the apostles' act of forming an official body of servants to care for the needy was bound to have lasting influence. It was a great plan that met a common need, and people are always eager to adapt good ideas to meet their needs. Thus it is reasonable to assume that the Seven became at least a prototype of later deacons.

A little more than one hundred years ago, the Anglican scholar, F. J. A. Hort (1828-1892), one of the most influential and brilliant biblical scholars of his day, commented:

> The Seven at Jerusalem would of course be well known to St Paul and to many others outside Palestine, and it would not be strange if the idea propagated itself. Indeed analogous wants might well lead to analogous institutions.[15]

As Hort says, "it would not be strange if the idea propagated itself." The problem of helping needy people was common to all the early churches, so the plan implemented by the Twelve and the church at Jerusalem would have been an appealing model for other churches to copy. It would have been most natural for other churches to duplicate what the apostles did in Jerusalem. In fact, that is precisely what churches of similar history and theology do today. They follow (sometimes slavishly, to their own detriment) the practices of their original congregation and its leaders.

By A.D. 62, the office of deacon was a recognized position with an official title in at least two churches established by Paul. As "a wise master builder" and church foundation layer (1 Corinthians 3:10), Paul is the most likely person to have propagated the Jerusalem model and given it permanent, universal status among the Gentile churches. Paul was in Jerusalem when the Seven were chosen and would have had many reasons to duplicate the Jerusalem model. He was concerned about organizational matters in the local congregation (Acts 14:23; 1 Timothy 3:1-13; 5:17-25; Titus 1:5-9). We know that he appointed a body of elders in most of the churches he planted (Acts 14:23), that he was deeply concerned about the poor (Acts 24:17; Galatians 2:10; Romans 15:25-27), and that he was concerned about certain uniform practices among the churches (1 Corinthians 4:17; 11:16). By implementing the practices of the Jerusalem church in new churches, Paul could foster a visible link between the Jerusalem and Gentile churches as well as solve common organizational problems.

To be sure, the New Testament diaconate had a beginning of significant origin. Church history reveals that the diaconate was an intrinsic part of every church throughout the Roman Empire, even during the earliest days of second-century Christianity. How do we explain its widespread, deep-rooted, and persistent nature? What better explanation is there than Acts 6 and the apostles' establishment of the Seven?

Whatever position one takes regarding the relationship between Acts 6 and the later deacons, the concept of deacons, as derived from Paul's two letters, is not altered. The office-title of deacon (*diakonos*) conveys the idea of practical care and service to others. Also, the fact that Scripture demands that deacons be morally qualified and examined before they serve (1 Timothy 3:8-13), tells us that their service would entail delicate matters of trust such as collecting and distributing the congregation's money and caring for people who have special needs.

Conspicuously absent in the deacon's list of requirements are the qualifications "able to teach" and "hospitable," which are both required of overseer-elders (1 Timothy 3:1-7). This shows that the office of deacon does not include teaching or official church leadership. Furthermore, the deacons' close association with the overseers indicates that their ministries are complementary. The overseers govern and teach; the deacons help to meet the many practical needs of needy people. Thus deacons certainly cannot go wrong in exploring this passages' rich storehouse of divine truths.

Part Two

A TWO-OFFICE CHURCH: OVERSEERS AND DEACONS

Now, dear Christians, some of you pray night and day to be branches of the true Vine; you pray to be made all over in the image of Christ. If so, you must be like him in giving. A branch bears the same kind of fruit as the tree.... An old divine says well: "What would have become of us if Christ had been as saving of his blood as some men are of their money?"

***Objection* 1. "My money is my own." *Answer*: Christ might have said, "My blood is my own, my life is my own"...then where should we have been?**

***Objection* 2. "The poor are undeserving." *Answer*: Christ might have said the same thing. "They are wicked rebels against my Father's law: shall I lay down my life for these? I will give to the good angels." But no, he left the ninety-nine, and came after the lost. He gave his blood for the undeserving.**

***Objection* 3. "The poor may abuse it." *Answer*: Christ might have said the same; yea, with far greater truth. Christ knew that thousands would trample his blood under their feet; that most would despise it...yet he gave his own blood.**

Oh, my dear Christians! If you would be like Christ, give much, give often, give freely, to the vile and the poor, the thankless and the undeserving. Christ is glorious and happy, and so will you be. It is not your money I want, but your happiness. Remember his own word: "It is more blessed to give than to receive."

Robert Murray McCheyne (1813-1843)
Sermon 82

Chapter 5

Overseers

Episkopoi

Paul and Timothy, bond-servants of Christ Jesus, to all the saints in Christ Jesus who are in Philippi, including the overseers and deacons.

Philippians 1:1

The first clear mention of deacons in the New Testament is found in Philippians 1:1. When Paul wrote his letter to the Philippians, he was under arrest in Rome. The Philippians dearly loved Paul, so while he was in custody in Rome (A.D. 60-62), they sent money and their personal envoy, Epaphroditus, to communicate their love and support for him.

This letter is unique in that Paul includes greetings to both the "overseers and deacons" in the opening salutation. The most likely reason the overseers and deacons are mentioned in the opening salutation is that they had a special part in initiating and organizing the church's financial contribution to Paul. Paul, therefore, acknowledges their special part. Of course, there may have been other reasons for greeting these church officials, but this seems to be the most obvious.

OVERSEERS

IDENTIFYING THE OVERSEERS

In the New Testament, deacons are always associated with overseers, yet are subordinate to and distinct from them. If we want to understand who the New Testament deacon is and what he does, we must begin with an understanding of the overseers of the church. If we misinterpret the identity of the New Testament overseers, we will most likely distort the identity of the New Testament deacons. In fact, in many churches today deacons act as if they are church overseers, which is not a New Testament teaching. Let us now consider the identity and duties of the New Testament overseer.

The Meaning of Episkopos

In the church at Philippi, there was a group called "overseers." The word *overseers* is derived from the Greek word *episkopos.* The following chart lays out the Greek and English words found in the New Testament that refer to church overseers.

English	**Greek**
overseer (or bishop)	*episkopos* (plural *episkopoi)*

• "And from Miletus he sent to Ephesus and called to him the elders of the church.... 'Be on guard for yourselves and for all the flock, among which the Holy Spirit has made you overseers [*episkopoi*], to shepherd [pastor] the church of God'" (Acts 20:17,28*a*).

• "Paul and Timothy, bond-servants of Christ Jesus, to all the saints in Christ Jesus who are in Philippi, including the overseers [*episkopoi*] and deacons" (Philippians 1:1).

• "An overseer [*episkopos*], then, must be above reproach" (1 Timothy 3:2*a*).

At night, there is a city's afterglow. There is a happiness in her solitude at dawn.

The leaf blows from her palm in another soft breeze. The watchful seagull struts the parapet, still hungry for crumbs that are not there. Someone stopped who need not have, and called an ambulance for Dumb Hanna when she lay senseless on the street. The ladies come at night with soup, well-meaning, never forgetting, no matter what the weather. The woman dentist said don't be in pain. The woman dentist has dedicated her existence to the rotten teeth of derelicts, to derelicts' odour and filth. Her goodness is a greater mystery than the evil that distorted a man's every spoken word, his every movement made. You would say it if you could, a new thought is, but sometimes saying isn't easy.

Idiot gawking, fool tramping nowhere: shreds of half-weary pity are thrown in the direction of a wayside figure, before the hasty glance darts on to something else. There will be other cities, and the streets of other cities, and other roads, Tappers and Georges and Lenas, Kevs and Davos and Dumb Hannas. There will be charity and shelter and mercy and disdain; and always, and everywhere, the chance that separates the living from the dead. Again the same people wander through her thoughts: the saint and the Little Sisters, Elsie Covington and Beth, Sharon and Gaye and Jakki and Bobbi, her mother not aged by a day. Are they really all together among the fragrant flowers, safe and blessed? She might be with them if it had happened; but she reflects, in modest doubt, that the certainty she knows is still what she would choose. She turns her hands so that the sun may catch them differently, and slightly lifts her head to warm the other side of her face.